EVELYN CUCCHIARA

30 Days To
An Organized Home

30 Days To An Organized Home

Quick, easy ways to spend less time getting more done at home.

Evelyn Cucchiara

ISBN: 1463716982
ISBN-9781463716981
Printed in the United States of America

DEDICATION

I'd like to dedicate this book to my wonderful IT Dept., also known as my husband Joe. Without him, this book would have stayed an idea in my head, or a document on my hard drive, never seeing the light of day. Thank you for doing the computer wizardry necessary to make this book real, and for supporting me throughout the thick and thin of it all.

I honestly could not have done it without you.

CONTENTS

ACKNOWLEDGMENTS

A great big thank you to Shelly for her invaluable help in editing my first copy and removing about a thousand dashes. And thank you to Regina, Sherry and Debbie for keeping us all moving forward towards our respective goals. And to think that it all started at lunch......

INTRODUCTION

I feel I know you.

Does this sound familiar? Do you spend way too much time trying to get your house in shape only to have it become a cluttered mess over and over again? I'm here to tell you it doesn't have to be that way. You need to work smarter, not harder. Harder gets you nowhere. Smarter gets you time to do what you want to do when you want to do it. And that's the goal of this book.

Long ago I realized that I have a talent. My talent is the ability to cut through the clutter of daily life, remove the obstacles and design and put in place systems to make sure the obstacles stay away forever.

I thought everyone had this talent.

Turns out they don't.

And not having this talent keeps people running around clearing the same clutter over and over, or doing the same tasks again and again, when they'd much rather be doing something else.

You now hold in your hands the key ending all that, the key to working smarter, not harder. You now have my systems that clear the clutter out of your life, keep your home running smoothly, and give you back your time.

All that time you spend looking for lost items, shoving things in closets, squishing just one more thing in one more place – that time could be spent doing much more enjoyable things – and that's probably why you're reading this. Wouldn't it be great if you could find what you were looking for in the first place you looked? Or bring home something from the store and actually have a place to store it?

If you are like most people, you wish you were more organized, but the task seems overwhelming. Where do you start? How can the mountains of clutter be scaled? The answer is in just a few minutes a day – little steps at a time. After all, Rome wasn't built in a day, but you can make major inroads in just a short amount of time. And once your house is more organized and running smoother, your mind will follow. It will get easier and easier to clean up, pare down and keep your home running smoother.

That's what this book is all about. It's here to help you, to get you to that happy place where your house works with you, not against you. Contained within its covers you will find time proven, best of the best, never fail systems to organize, streamline and make your home more efficient. And they work. They've been tested in the trenches.

Here are my trenches:
I have three boys.
And two cats.

And for twelve years I've owned a home based business that has dozens of people going in and out of my home every day. With small children. And messy art projects.

And I run a business doing organizing consultations focusing on home efficiency.

And I blog about organizing. You can check out my blog at http://www.allevelyn.com.

And I run an organic food co-op out of my garage every other week.

Those are my trenches. Sounds busy, right? It is, but since designing and using my systems, my life runs smoothly. My house is ready for anything,

Need examples? Here you go...... My husband and I host parties almost every month, socialize with friends all the time – and our house is always neat, clean and user friendly. I cook dinner every night. We clean our own house, no cleaning ladies here. Granted, our house isn't huge, it's a Cape Cod style home, but every part of it is usable. Week after week, year after year, all runs smoothly because our home is organized with systems that work with us, not against us. Every idea I give you is something I actually use. Time tested, family approved, useful information.

And let's set the record straight, right from the start.

It is impossible to organize your entire house in a day. So don't set that unattainable goal for yourself.

You may be able to get your house cleaned up, but it will never stay that way. What is possible, is to get started with small steps, one at a time.

And that's how this book is organized. It is divided up into small sections so you can tackle it day by day. 30 days, 30 different sections of ideas for different areas of your home that seem to attract clutter and mess. Within each section, I describe in great detail tips and systems that will make your life easier, scout's honor. And a place for notes in the back. I want you to use this book as a tool, so mark up the pages, jot down to do lists.

I've also included a few quick easy ideas to help you get started. Don't worry, none of the tips will be too complicated or time consuming. Just fun, easy and life changing. I'll end with proven ways to keep your newly organized home organized. Because, after all, if you can't keep your new systems and procedures going after you set them up – what good are they to you?

Ready? Let's get started......

Five Easy Tips To Live By:

1. If you take it out, put it away.

2. If you use it up, refill it or throw it away.

3. If it doesn't bring you happiness and joy each time you look at it, get rid of it.

4. If you can't use it, give it away.

5. If you haven't used it in a year, get rid of it.

Memorize these. Copy them on to a small piece of paper you keep in your wallet. Post them on your calendar.

Live your life by these simple guidelines and I guarantee you will never be drowning in stuff.

But first, you have to get rid of some stuff, so on to the nuts and bolts of how to do just that......

As I said before, this book is divided up into sections just like your house. This way you can bite off one room at a time in order to make sense of your clutter.

The sections are:

1. THE KITCHEN
2. THE BATHROOM
3. THE BEDROOMS
4. THE ENTRYWAY
5. THE LIVING ROOM / FAMILY ROOM
6. THE GREAT OUTDOORS
7. THE THINGS THAT DON'T FIT INTO ANY OTHER CATEGORY

Let's start with the room you probably spend most of your time in –

1. THE KITCHEN

Okay – as we all know, if the kitchen is a mess, nothing can get done. Food doesn't get cooked, the piles get bigger, it feels like everything is about to come crashing down on you, both literally and figuratively. So, let's get started......

Day 1 - Kitchen Counters

Let's start with the obvious – keep your kitchen counters clean!

No knick-knacks, no cute baskets, no piles of incoming mail! If it doesn't have an exact purpose, if it's not something you use every day, it has no business being on your counter. For now, grab a bag or basket and dump all of the paper you see on your counters into it. This includes mail, schoolwork, newspapers – whatever you have stacked up. Throw it all into a bag (or bags if needed) and vow to go through it next time you are sitting around watching some mindless television. However, don't go through the pile until we've set up a way to handle it! For now, just put it somewhere out of the kitchen, but not where you'll trip over it. And make sure it is out of sight.

Okay – what else is on the counter – see any medicines, vitamins, anything like that? Yes, you may use these every day, but they do not belong on the counter where everyone can see them and possibly a child may find them. Get a basket or box or something where they can all be together and put them in there. Make sure it's small enough to fit into a kitchen cabinet, because that's where their new home is going to be. In addition, be sure you only have out what you actually take - anything old and expired needs to be disposed of. An alternative way to store vitamins is to get a wall spice shelf and store them in decorative jars. That way they can be accessible, but not look like clutter. I found a terrific one at a garage sale that I use – it's mounted on the wall right next to the kitchen table. The kid's vitamins are stored in separate jars for each child. That way they can easily grab them and take them in the morning. That works great for vitamins, prescriptions are better off stored in their original containers in a cabinet – either kitchen or bathroom, whichever works best for you.

Great! Now – what else is on your counter? Any food products should be stored away. More on that later. For now, take the food and put it in a cabinet somewhere.

You should be left with assorted things – eyeglasses, kid's toys, electronic equipment, etc. Remove whatever doesn't belong in the kitchen and bring it to whatever room it belongs in. What's left on the counters? Any appliances you use daily can stay – (coffee maker, blender, toaster) – anything you use less than daily should be stored away. My counter has a toaster, coffee maker, fruit bowl, knife block, dish drainer, cookie jar and "decorative chest". I use these things every day, so they've earned their spot on the counter. Even though I bake almost every day, I keep my mixer in the cabinet below. I just don't like the look of it sitting on the counter. Same for the food processor, blender, pressure cooker and crock-pot. I use them often, but I still keep them stored away – yet handy to get to.

Now – you may be wondering why I keep a decorative chest on my counter. It's one of my favorite organizing tools! It's big, easy to open and nice to look at – and I keep all sorts of papers in there! It's known as "the treasure chest" in my house, and any incoming paperwork goes in there , including: papers from the kid's backpacks that need to be filled out, interesting articles from magazines, recipes I've clipped, odd papers that I don't know if they are important or not because they're not mine (after all, there are 5 people living in this house!), paperwork for upcoming events like parties, bills that need to be paid – you get the idea. I also put pages from magazines about interesting places to go, restaurants to try, holiday ideas and such.

Every day I go through the mail, recycle what I can, and anything that needs further attention goes in the chest. Kid's paperwork from their backpack – anything that needs me to follow up on goes into the chest. Small cables, etc. that I have no idea what they are – into the chest they go. My chest is about 8 inches high – so it can hold a good amount of stuff – definitely a weeks' worth. And this is important since I only go through it once a week to take care of the paperwork in it. Only takes a few minutes - here's what I do. Open the chest and sort the contents into piles such as keep in the box, recycle, husband's stuff, bills, file, school, - whatever piles work for you. Then – act on the piles. Bills I pay, filing gets done, (things like insurance paperwork, trip ideas, and recipes. More on this later). It's important to empty the chest once a week and put back into it only things that are pending. Don't just fill it up with junk!

I must admit though, it's amazing how often the things I save at the beginning of the week become recyclable by the end of the week. Did I really think I was going to make a tofu recipe? And speaking of recipes, I keep cut out ones in the chest all clipped together. I try to make the recipes within a few weeks of clipping them. If not, I discard them – figuring it wasn't meant to be. If I've made it and the family likes it, I file it away. (More about that under paperwork.) If we don't like it, the recipe goes into recycling.

Okay – your kitchen counters should be looking a lot cleaner by now. Keep that treasure chest or box handy – it will be a lifesaver for collecting all of that paperwork that otherwise would end up on your counter! Take a deep breath – you're making progress! Don't you feel more in control already? Great job so far!

Day 2 – Kitchen Cabinets

Now let's look at the cabinets themselves. What's in them? First, let's examine the dish cabinets. Open them up and take everything out. Now – all you really need is one set of everyday dishes. I personally like Corelle, because they stack easily, and when you drop them they don't break. I also have a set of china, but it's stored away for special occasions. And yes, I do use them quite a few times a year. Mine are stored in the basement, but not in boxes, just stacked on shelves so I can easily get them when I need them. If you have a big kitchen with lots of storage, feel free to store your china there – my kitchen is too small. And, the point is to have your "good" china accessible, but not in a cabinet you use every day. If you happen to have holiday china, I would suggest donating it somewhere. Do you really need an entire set of dishes with Christmas trees on them?

Now, it's time to put your dishes back into the cabinet, but first go and buy some wire racks that you can stack plates and such on. Make the most out of your cabinet space. This is what my cabinet looks like – bottom shelf holds small plates, small bowls, soup bowls, saucers, cups, and dinner plates. All easy to get to, and more important, easy to put away. The cabinet is located right above the dishwasher so steps aren't wasted when putting dishes away. Next shelf holds coffee mugs, ramekins, anything we use often. Top shelf holds pitchers, special dishes, things I use, but not every day.

Glasses are stored in a different cabinet – again – just what we use. I'd donate all of your mismatched glasses and buy a durable set for everyday use. Figure out how many you need, and get a set that fits your family. 12 small glasses and 12 large glasses seem to work for us. Don't worry about having extras for entertaining right now, we'll discuss that later.

What else are you storing? Pots, pans baking dishes? Again, figure out what you use, get rid of the extra, and put the ones you need in a handy spot. I have a set of stainless steel pans. I use one small frying pan, one large one, one really large one like a wok size (I use this one the most), one small pot, one large pot and one pasta pot. That's it. These are the ones I use the most, so this is what I have. I'm all for having one pot or pan be able to handle many recipes. That's why I made sure that my pots and pans can go into the oven also (no non heat safe handles). I've also given up on nonstick cookware. They just don't last long enough! The set I have now is from Cuisinart – and I love it! It's easy to use, easy to keep clean! I store my mixer in the same cabinet as my pots, right under my main work counter, easy to get to. Large mixing bowls are also here. Again, pare down what you don't need! Since I bake a lot, I have a large plastic bowl with a handle, the bowl for my mixer, and two glass bowls that can also be used for serving. That's it. If I don't use something once a month, it doesn't live in my kitchen. It's amazing how many kitchen gadgets you don't need! And always remember a sharp knife is your most useful tool......

Another cabinet holds the food processor, plastic food storage cubes (more about this later), flower vases, my Vita-Mix blender, aluminum foil for packing sandwiches, and wax paper squares for baking and packaging. The small cabinet over the range hood holds each family members' refillable water bottle, a few large glass goblets, and insulted coffee mugs. My last remaining cabinet holds serving platters, & cookie sheets – all stored on their sides to take up less space and make them easy to get to. And that's it for dish/pot/pan storage. I do have a few special pans for cakes and pies, but since I don't use those more than once a month, they are stored in a hall closet. Close to the kitchen, but not taking up valuable space.

Done with Day 2 – hooray!

Day 3 – Food Storage

Now what about food storage? In my kitchen above the glasses, I have all the cereals, crackers, pretzels, and nuts (dry stuff we use all the time). However, none of it is stored in their original boxes. Instead, in order to take up less space, they are each stored in a separate, stackable bin. The stackable bins are long and shallow – kind of like a large shoebox. They have snap on lids that makes it easy for the kids to help themselves, keeps the contents fresh, and takes up less space in the cabinet. All the boxes are labeled on both ends with the contents, this way no matter which way the box slides back in, you can still tell what's in it. In addition, I store a scoop or spoon inside each one to make serving easier.

Baking items like flour and sugar are stored in decorative glass canisters on a shelving unit we put next to the refrigerator. We simply installed triangle shelves in the unused space there and made a mini bakers rack out of it. And keeping baking ingredients handy makes baking up a batch of brownies much easier! The kids each have a glass canister on the triangle rack that stores their candy from holidays and such. That way no fighting about whose candy is whose.

Other food articles are stored in a small closet off the kitchen. All types of pasta are in a basket, snack items are in another basket, and canned goods are on a shallow shelf inside the closet door. Only store what you need, and use up what you have before buying more. Store like items together so you know what you have! Spices are stored in a cabinet next to the stove – easy to get to when cooking. Knowing where something is makes cooking much easier.

Down in the basement I have a very large, full size, upright freezer. This makes it easy to stock up on items like bread and ice cream when they are on sale. I also store all of my meat in here. I buy from a service that sells all organic meat, and they come to your house twice a year to stock your freezer. This makes it simple to organize meals and plan ahead. No last minute trips to the supermarket for us. I'd much rather use that time to read a book! And you always have food on hand for last minute guests......On to the next day!

Day 4 – Meal Planning

Meal planning – I can't stress enough how much time, money and effort you can save by planning out your meals a week in advance. Now I know some of you will say that it's impossible, but give it a try. Spend a few minutes on a Sunday morning with a cup of coffee, figuring out what you will be making this week. The rewards will be tenfold.

Here's how I do it. First, sit down with some scrap paper. (I tear all of our scrap paper into fourths and hold them together with a clip, so we always have some around.) Anyway, get three pieces of paper. On one, write these headings vertically down the left side: beef/pork, chicken, fish, veggie, chicken, fish, clean out fridge. This will give you seven meals. Then, take stock of what you have on hand. What's in your freezer? What's on your shelves? I'm a member of an organic food co-op, so I'm always asking what veggies and fruits do I need to use up before the next delivery?

Next, flip through cookbooks, look at recipes you've taken out of magazines, and go to the internet to find ideas. Come up with a menu idea for each of the headings using what you have on hand. Then fill in the blanks. When you are done, you'll have one beef/pork meal, two chicken meals, two fish meals, one veggie meal, and one clean out the fridge meal. This way you're not eating too much beef, and you're getting enough fish. Remember to add side dishes also.

While you are doing this, make a shopping list on one of the other pieces of paper, add any ingredients you need to buy for the recipes. Now, consult your calendar and see what your upcoming week holds. Will you be home each night for dinner? Do you need a quick dinner on the night you have a meeting? On your last piece of paper, write the days of the week down the left side. Fill in the meals you have planned for each, taking into account what you have going on that day/night. Plan accordingly. Once your days of the week list is all filled in, you'll have a list of food for the week. It's easy to consult this list the day before so you know if you have to thaw something out – no surprises. And, if you have a spare few minutes during your day, you can start the prep work for that day's dinner. I often chop whatever veggie I need in the morning, that way it's all ready to go.

Now – where to put those lists so you don't lose them? This leads us to one of the greatest, underused areas of the kitchen –

Day 5 - Inside of the Cabinet Doors

The inside of your cabinet doors. What's inside your cabinet doors? Go take a look. Is it just unused space? If so, you are missing out on one of the greatest organization spaces! I have six doors at chest height in my kitchen. Here's what's inside of mine -

The first door has a list of what time each of the boy's school starts, what time the boys need to get on the bus, the time for delayed openings, a CPR flyer (just in case), and the phone number for poison control, (again, just in case)

The second door has our family calendar. This is as large as the door, and has spaces big enough to write everything on. I like to keep it inside the door so it's not out for all to see, reducing visual clutter in the kitchen. Having it inside the door makes it easily accessible, but not right in my face. I also keep a pen on the shelf right next to the dishes so it's easy to add items. And we only have one calendar, not one I carry around with me, not an electronic one, just one old fashioned paper one hanging where everyone in the family knows where it is. I can easily consult it every morning to see what's going on that day, as well as check it when planning weekly meals.

The third door has motivational ideas, quotes, sayings, and things just for me. It's uplifting to have these around, and inside this cabinet I usually stumble upon them without meaning to.

The fourth door has a cute tile my first son made for Fathers Day's years ago, and a large envelope that stores preprinted shopping lists for the food stores I go to. I create these lists on the computer and arrange the items on the list the same way the store is laid out. I fill in the items we buy regularly, and then print out ten at a time. When I know I need something from a specific store, I check it off on the appropriate list. I have them made for Trader Joe's, Shop Rite, and Costco. This way if I am going, I can consult the list and see if I am running low on anything else so I can pick it up while I am there, saving trips to the store. Alternatively, if my husband will be in the vicinity of the store that day, I give him the list so he can stop by. Since the items are listed in the order they are in the store, it's easy for anyone to follow it. My shopping list from meal planning gets transcribed to these lists also. I have a clothespin like clip clipped to the envelope for any coupons I have. This way I can't forget them because they are right in front of the lists.

The fifth door has a letter size envelope containing any recipes I need for that week (from meal planning), and a meals for the week list clipped to the outside of the envelope. I work on the theory that if I can write it down, I don't need to remember it! Why rethink the same info over and over again? Also in that vein, I have a list posted inside this door of whose laundry needs to get done on what day. I can never seem to remember that!

The sixth door has a built in spice rack. The house came that way, but I use it all the time. If you can fit one inside your cabinet door, I strongly suggest it!

That's it, not much really, but it helps keep track of things in an easily accessible place without adding to the overall clutter. And it uses a space that is usually ignored.

Time to make your appliances do some of the work......

Day 6 – Time Saving Appliances

Next on the list are things that can take the place of you (well, not really, but every little bit helps!).

My favorite idea is to have a menu board in your kitchen. Why you may ask? Are you running a restaurant? Is it just something to look cute? Not at all. It's one of the greatest sanity saving devices ever invented! Why? Because it keeps you from answering the "Mom, what's for dinner?" question at least a million times a day! If your family is anything like mine, no matter how many times I tell them what's for dinner, it never registers. The solution? A simple 6" x 8" white ceramic tile from the hardware store.

Every morning (sometimes the night before) I write DINNER on the top with a washable marker, then underneath list what's for dinner. For example, it may say

– meat loaf, potatoes, carrots, apples. Whatever you are having, all parts of it, list it on the board. Remember – right inside your kitchen cabinet you have a posted list, all you have to do is transcribe it over to the board for that day. Presto, no one asks you anymore! And, since it's written down, no one will argue with it. For some strange reason, once it's written down, family members think it's written in stone, and no one questions it. It also serves the secondary purpose of when you are getting dinner ready, to check the menu board and make sure you haven't forgotten anything. And it just makes you feel on top of things. After all, if your dinner is already planned out and posted, how disorganized could the rest of your life be? At least it keeps the illusion going! I keep it propped up on the kitchen windowsill. Each night I just rinse it off under the kitchen faucet and it's clean and ready to go for the next day. I usually fill it in at breakfast time.

Another great underused item is the delayed start button on your oven. Does yours have one? Do you even know? Go check, because if it does, you are missing out on a great time saver. For example, I used it last night. I made the casserole for dinner while the kids were having snack after school. Instead of putting it in the refrigerator and then coming back later to put it in the oven and turn it on, I simply put the dish into the oven and set the oven to start in a half hour. Then I went and got my book and sat down to read. I didn't need to report back to the kitchen until 15 minutes before the casserole was ready. Then I just assembled the remaining items for dinner. And, I set my kitchen timer to tell me when 15 minutes before dinner was so I didn't have to keep checking the clock. I could read in peace, knowing that my appliances were doing their jobs without any help from me. I used it again today when I put a sweet potato in the oven for lunch at 9:30 am, set the oven to go on at 11:00 so when I finished teaching my art class, lunch was ready. A minute of planning ahead made lunch something to look forward to – without any real effort from me. Now, use good sense and don't put something in there hours before the oven turns on, but a short amount of time is fine.

If you need to start dinner really early in the day, that leads us to another great invention to take the place of you, the crock-pot. You probably have one stored somewhere. Dig it out and use it! Just don't store it on your kitchen counter making more clutter. Mine lives on a shelf in the basement where I can easily get it, but it's not something I see every day. If you have no idea what to cook in it, just look up crock pot recipes on line. There are zillions of them. The crock pot is great for things like pot roast, chili, and soups. I even found a terrific macaroni and cheese recipe for it, starting with dry macaroni. Nothing better than coming in the house right at dinner time and dinner's ready and waiting for you.

If you have a day on your schedule when you are out of the house right up to dinnertime, add a crock-pot recipe to the menu for that day. It couldn't be easier! Just put everything inside in the morning, plug it in, turn it on, and look forward to a great dinner when you get home. Just remember to plug it in! One time I made a meatloaf, put it in the crock-pot, and went to visit a friend for the day. When I got home, I realized I had turned it on, but I didn't plug it in. Needless to say, since the raw meat was sitting out all day, the whole thing went into the trash. I think we had pizza that night......

Have you ever used a pressure cooker? Another great invention, and well worth its cost. The modern ones are safe and fool proof. They cook under pressure, so food is cooked quickly and thoroughly. One time I invited a friend and her family to dinner, then cooked chili from frozen ground beef while the friend and I had a glass of wine. The chili was done, the flavors were blended, all in the time it took to drink a glass of wine. Again, look up recipes on the internet. I use it all the time to make chicken stock from roast chicken leftovers, soften dried beans and stews. Almost anything you can cook in a pot you can make faster and easier with a pressure cooker.

Another appliance that frees up your time is a high-speed blender. I got a Vita-Mix a few years ago, and it's become one of those appliances I didn't know I needed until I had it. Now I don't know how I lived without it. I use it a least once a day to make fruit smoothies, and soups, using up extra veggies. My teenager likes a smoothie each day. Using the vita mix, I throw in a banana, a whole apple, some carrots, some frozen fruit and ice cubes, push a button, and in seconds I have a perfectly smooth smoothie. And lots of it! I store it in the fridge, and he drinks it all during the day. In addition, if I have extra cooked veggies from dinner, I can blend them the next day with a bit of broth or milk and make soup for lunch.

Right now, I have a pot of soup I made from leftover roasted veggies from the other night, including beets. Now, I've learned I don't really like beets, but they're fine in soup. I've been having a cup as a mid-afternoon snack for a few days and it's great. It's very healthy, delicious and easy. Just the other night I was making spaghetti and meatballs, and I had a zucchini I needed to use up. I put it in the Vita mix with a bit of sauce, hit on, and then poured it into the pot of sauce. It added extra nutrition, got rid of leftovers, and the kids ate it all. If I had put a zucchini in front of them, none of them would have touched it. It was healthy and cleaned out the fridge at the same time – can't beat that! And speaking of the fridge.....

Day 7 – Refrigerator

Okay, how about your refrigerator? Is it helping you or not? Here are some things I've added to mine to make life easier. I put a Lazy Susan on the condiment shelf. All those little jars and bottles go on there – mustard, jelly, cream cheese, etc. You can spin it, so you can see what you have. A bin just for cheese sticks is in the door. We buy them at Costco – then we open the package and put them into the bin on the door. This way the kids can easily grab them. Easy to get to and healthy too. Kind of like taking the cereal out of the box.

Leftover shelf – the top shelf always holds leftovers – that way nothing gets lost in the fridge, and you know what you need to use up. And when someone's hungry, they can see what's available. (Just remember, if you are planning to use something for a recipe – put a sticky note on it so no one eats it accidently. Or if you want it for lunch, put a note on it too!)

And while we are in the refrigerator – let's talk about milk and juice. Know how to cut out those trips to the store for milk and juice? A milkman! See if your area has home milk delivery. Now, I know you think I'm kidding, but check it out on line. More and more areas have it, it just remains a big secret. We've had a milkman for over a dozen years. And yes, it's just like you think. He comes in the early dawn and leaves the milk and juice in the box by my front door. No, the milk doesn't come in glass bottles, but you can't have everything.

Anyway, I get deliveries once a week (used to be twice a week when the kids were smaller). He delivers milk and orange juice, but I could also get butter, eggs, yogurt, and all sorts of things. Now I admit, it does cost more than at the store, but I figure for the time it saves me, as well as the lack of impulse buys I make when just running to the store for milk, I'm still coming out ahead. And I never run out of milk! And just in case I run out of juice, I always stock the fixings for lemonade. No, not a mix, I just add 1 cup of lemon juice from a big bottle, (Costco), and 1 cup of sugar to a pitcher or water, mix and voila – lemonade. No artificial ingredients and no corn syrup either. Couldn't be easier.

Day 8 – Miscellaneous Kitchen Ideas

Okay, I think that's it for the kitchen, no wait, I also store the cat food in a decorative wood bin right next to their bowls. That way anyone can feed the cats. I just dump the big bag of dry food right into the bin. It's easy, quick and neat.   It probably wouldn't work with dogs though, you would need a locking bin for them. We also get water delivered in 5-gallon bottles and have an old-fashioned water cooler in the corner. We never run out and there aren't any bottles to recycle.

I also have an old desk with glass doors on top in the kitchen where I store cookbooks. That way the books are easily accessible. The trash can is under the kitchen sink on a roll out shelf. When you open the door, it slides out. You can get it at a hardware store. The recycling bin is next to the trash can. Please don't store your trash can and recycling bin where they're visible. It just makes the kitchen look messy.

I also use a thin stretchy thread, like elastic, strung up horizontally against the wall for hanging greeting cards. It's a 6 foot long length of almost invisible thread held up by two nails. It's easy to hang greeting cards sideways over the thread; they don't fall off, and it's simple to get them down. It's strong enough that you can overlap the cards too, so it can hold all of the holiday cards. The photo cards we get I attach all in one place on the thread with a clothespin-like clip. And when there are no cards, the thread springs back up and you can't even see it!

I have a metal wire basket that is attached to the water cooler by the phone. It holds the address book, scrap paper, and school phone books. A recycled tin can, covered with decorative paper, is foam taped to the wall and holds pens and pencils. Oh, I almost forgot the dinner bell! We picked up an old-fashioned wall mount bell while on vacation one year. We mounted it in the kitchen, and whenever dinner is ready, I ring it. It's much easier than shouting and everyone hears it. Done!

2. THE BATHROOM

Whether big or small, the bathroom holds its own set of challenges. We have two, and they are really small, so organization is the key here. My downstairs bathroom has a tiny bit of built in storage, but it's never enough. It seems no matter how much storage you have, it's never enough. Especially if it's not well organized. Here are my ideas for one of the busiest places in the house......

Day 9 – Bathroom Storage

Divide and conquer with bins and baskets. Bathroom storage is usually minimal, so you need to be ruthless. My cabinet has four shelves. Each shelf holds a basket, kind of like a small laundry basket. The basket on the first shelf holds toiletries, hair brushes, lotions, etc. Anything that's not medicine goes in that basket. Go through all you have and get rid of whatever you don't use or has expired. Put whatever you have left back in the basket, and label the basket. I use the handy label makers they sell at Staples.

The second shelf has medicines. Again, go through everything you have, and toss whatever has expired or that you don't use. Try to streamline. Do you really need five different pain killers or will one type do? Remember, if you can't find it, you won't use it, so make it easy to see. Label the basket, and be sure to keep it out of small children's reach.

The third shelf has a small bin for batteries (open the packages when you buy them and put them in the bin), and a basket for light bulbs. The bin keeps the bulbs safe and less likely to fall......

The top shelf holds a basket with what I call "health machines", like thermometers, blood pressure readers, ice packs, etc. Again, label everything it so family members can find what they need without you.

That's all that's in the cabinet. Notice there are no towels, no toilet paper, and no tissues. All those items are kept in a centrally located closet upstairs. A small supply of toilet paper is kept in a special rack that mounts next to the toilet, out of sight but easily accessible when needed.

Under the sink I keep the following, (on a special roll out shelf that makes it easy to get to) toilet cleaner, glass cleaner, wipes, toilet brush, and a sponge. All the cleaners are nontoxic, so it's safe to store them under the sink. That's it. Don't cram things under there because you will never be able to put them back. A good rule of thumb for storing anything from tools to toys is to make it all harder to get out then put back. You're more motivated to spend an extra few seconds taking something out than putting it away. So work with that natural tendency and make things easy to put away.

The upstairs bathroom has versions of the same. It has a small basket for toiletries, and one for medicines. One small, low closet is used just to store toilet paper and tissues. That way I can buy them in bulk and never run out. Toothbrushes and toothpaste are stored in a basket on the back of the toilet. A bit difficult to sort through and remove the right one, but very easy to toss back in the basket when done. An alternative that I saw at a friend's house is to store the toothbrushes horizontally on the inside of the medicine cabinet door, supported by two adhesive hooks. There they are easy to get to, but not out for everyone to see. And speaking of medicine cabinets, only store items you use every day. The medicine cabinet is not the place for Band-Aids, shampoo or jewelry. My makeup is stored in a small basket in the bathroom closet. Band-Aids are stored in a small decorative metal tin on a shelf. That way family members can get to them easily. And a small tub of first aid cream should also be stored in the box with the Band-Aids.

Now, what about all the shampoo, conditioner, bubble bath, and bath toys you may ask? They can all be stored in one of my favorite inventions – a shower curtain with interior pockets! Basically, it's a shower curtain liner, but it has built in clear pockets that hold all those things you need in the shower. Hang it up, stuff the pockets, hang a decorative curtain in front and voila, no more clutter in the bathroom. Plus, it makes the room super easy to clean! Don't forget to replace your hair dryer with a wall mount version. There are no plugs to deal with, and it's always ready when you are.

Earrings, rings, and such can go into small bowls that are on a shelf. They are easy to put your jewelry into when you take it off and earrings and such won't be falling off a shelf and on to the floor. Remember to empty it once a week, or all your jewelry could end up in there instead of a jewelry box. Just look at your bathroom as if it was a public place – because sometimes it is! What would you not want people to see?

And one last very important item for the bathroom, a clock. Make it something that looks good as well as works well. It's easy to keep yourself on schedule when you can see what time it is.

That's it for the bathrooms. Moving right along, next up are the bedrooms......

3. THE BEDROOMS

There's nothing more depressing than waking up in a room filled with last nights, last weeks or last year's clutter. How can you possibly get out of bed if that's what's facing you? Time to do something about it for good! You wake up feeling energized and ready to go when your bedroom is working with you, not against you.

Day 10 – Floor Space

Floor space - Clutter can take over a bedroom in a matter of minutes if you let it. The goal is to make your bedroom a calm and peaceful place, so try and remove anything that doesn't fall into that category. That means if you don't use the exercise bike in there, get it out. Computers really shouldn't be there either. All those tiny lights and constantly running energy does not make for peaceful sleeping.

Since our bedroom is small, I make sure that all side tables have built in storage. The more drawers, the better. Next to my side of the bed is a four drawer chest. It takes up no more room than an open end table, but provides places to store glasses, hand cream, books, chap stick and anything that would normally be needed and possibly left out to add clutter to the room. This way the top of the chest only has my jewelry box, a clock and a lamp. It is easy to dust, and easy to find things.

We also fit two small-upholstered chairs in our room. It makes for another place you can get away from the hustle and bustle of the family. We also use it for family reading time before the kids go to bed. Now, keep in mind these chairs are not huge. They are scaled to the room and fit perfectly. They are a great use of space. In addition, between them is a cabinet that was originally a small wood file cabinet. The cabinet makes a great divider between the chairs, and it's big enough for the phone, a lamp, and a few current magazines. Inside the file cabinet drawers we store additional magazines (what can I say, some members of my family like to hoard things), and a small blanket in case anyone gets cold while reading.

My husband and I share one dresser that fits exactly into the eave space, so in reality it sits flush with the wall. We have one other eave space that contains a window. That has a low table in it that holds baskets for my husband to empty his pockets into, and various decorative items. Usually these have a dual purpose also, such a as a vase that was an anniversary present holding loose change. All family photos are mounted on the wall – less to dust around. The only other item that takes up floor space is the bed – but that has storage under it – so it doesn't really count!

Day 11 – Closets

Our bedroom only has two very small closets. They are built into the roof line, so they aren't even full size closets. We live in a Cape Cod style home, so you can picture what I mean. The closets in our bedroom are only about 3 feet wide, about 2 ½ feet deep and only 6 feet tall (with a sloping back). As I said, these are small closets. My husband is 6'2", and I'm 5'6", so you can imagine that not much fits in these. Organization is a must. Now, I do have an additional closet out in the hall, but it's probably smaller than the one in my bedroom. We also have a deep closet in the hall that is used for winter coats, suits and motorcycle gear, but the bulk of our clothing is stored in these three closets. So, it is imperative that what is kept in each one is well organized.

What are the secrets to storing your wardrobe in a tiny space? Well, first off, get rid of anything that doesn't fit you right now. If you are planning to lose weight, and something doesn't fit you now, it shouldn't be taking up valuable space. I would get rid of it, but if you feel you must keep some items, box them up, label them, and store them in some out of the way place. Next, remove whatever isn't in season right now. It makes no sense keeping wool sweaters easily accessible in the middle of July. Box them up, label them, and get them out of there.

Now what's left? Hopefully things you actually wear. Here's a great way to find out how often you wear something. Once you put your clothes on hangers, hang them back in your closet with the hook facing out, or, backwards. When you take something out to wear, hang it back up with the hanger facing the regular way. After three months, see what hangers are still backwards. Those are the items that for some reason or another you don't wear. So, get rid of them. And the best way to get rid of them is to donate them. It's a win/win situation for everyone.

Now your closet should have some breathing room. But you want to make sure that it doesn't become clogged again soon. So, in order to avoid that, stick to this simple rule. Whenever you get something new, get rid of something else. It sounds harsh, but it works! This way you never run out of hangers either.

Now what about shoes? The same rules apply to shoes as they do to clothes. Just keep what you wear. And keep out of season shoes somewhere else. Store the shoes you wear in some sort of a shoe holder. Throwing shoes on the floor of the closet doesn't work. It should because it follows the rule of making it harder to get out then put back, but it just doesn't work. Maybe it's too dark to see inside?

Just put up some hooks, and you're all set. They are easy to get to, and easy to use. On the back of my other closet door, I hung a square carpet sample, with cup hooks hung above. The hooks hold my necklaces, and the carpet square keeps them from clacking against the door. The result? The necklaces are easy to see and access.

On the outside of the closet door hang up some sort of decorative hook. Here you can hang the clothes you need to air out overnight before they go back into your closet. The next morning, just put them away. No clutter, no muss, no fuss.

On to the next hurdle......

Day 12 – Laundry

Laundry – how can you possibly keep on top of it? It's easy, just set up a schedule and keep to it. Now, everybody has different ideas about how often things need to be laundered. So, I'll tell you what I do, and it may or may not work for your family. The important thing is to understand exactly what your family needs in the way of laundry, and create a schedule that works for you.

I personally am a morning person. Asking me to sort, wash, dry and fold laundry at night is an impossible dream. So, I take advantage of when I have most of my energy, and plan our laundry around that. Here's how it works......

We have five people in our family. My husband and I keep a laundry basket in the bottom of the linen closet. Our laundry goes in there. My two younger sons, 10 and

12, share a room. They have a laundry basket in their closet too. Their laundry baskets is up on a shelf so that they can shoot baskets when they take their clothes off at the end of the day. It makes it more fun for them, and clothes are never left lying around their room. My older son, a teen, has a basket in his room also. Notice I say "baskets", not hampers. What we use are your standard plastic laundry baskets. This way I don't have to empty a hamper, I just carry the entire basket downstairs.

Each of us gets our laundry done twice a week. I don't have to do much sorting since no one on my house wears white. I just throw all the clothes in together, shirts with jeans, etc. I will separate the clothes if there seems to be a lot of extra clothes that week, but in general, whatever is in the laundry basket goes into the same load. This might not work for some families. It depends on what you are comfortable with. It works for us!

My older son usually has a smaller load, but he's 6'4", and a teenager, so he goes through a lot of laundry. Our schedule works like this: Sunday – younger sons, Monday – my husband and I, Tuesday, - older son, Wednesday – household – Thursday – younger sons, Friday – us, Sat – older son. You get it? Everyone has two days a week allotted to them. This schedule seems to get the clothes washed in a timely manner. And, if all your family members have cleaned their closets out, they won't have that many extra items of clothing taking up space in their closets.

Now, for the actual washing part of the system. As I said, I'm not a night person, but I can put the laundry, detergent, and softener in the machine right before I go to sleep. Then I set the washer to start at 4:00 in the morning. Most washers today have the ability to delay the start. I bet you wondered what in the world you would ever use the delay start for. Well, here's the answer. It's a terrific time saver! Set up the laundry the night before, the washer turns on while you are sleeping and when you wake up, just toss everything in the dryer. Setting the wash to start two hours before you wake up – (I get up at 6:00 am), means the laundry isn't sitting there wet and getting wrinkled for hours. And you won't forget to put it in the dryer. When I come downstairs in the morning, the first thing I do is put the laundry into the dryer, then feed the cats, kids, etc.

Before I know it, the laundry is dry. And what also works for me is to put the folding of the laundry right into my usual morning routine. Right now it's working for me to fold my laundry around 7:30, right after my first two sons leave for school, and while my third son is practicing his violin. I fold right next to him. Because it is part of our routine, it reminds him to practice and it reminds me to fold laundry. Once finished, I immediately go upstairs and put the laundry away.

Doing the laundry early in the morning, before anyone (including me) is awake, completely eliminates that problem of someone's shower water getting too hot while the washer is running. No one is awake – so no one notices the water temperature change. The laundry is all clean, folded, and put away before 8:00 am. Now, every once in a while, something delays it. For example, this morning I got up a bit later, so the laundry wasn't yet dry when my youngest was practicing his violin. But overall, it does work and makes it one less thing you need to think about throughout the day. As long as you keep to the schedule, you don't need to waste brainpower on it over and over.

Day 13 – Your Clothing

Clothing – how much is too much? There is no sense trying to organize a closet that is too full of clothes. You might make it work for a week, but before you know it, it will be a mess again. So, you need to pare down, and not just you, but your entire family. However, I wouldn't waste my time trying to organize my teen. I just set a good example and hope for the best. Just be sure their room has a door on it that closes tightly so you don't have to see the mess. Pick your battles very carefully there! But for the rest of us, paring down works. As I already mentioned above, when you get something new, get rid of something old. Remember to hang your hangers backwards so you know what you don't wear. But, it can't hurt to start with less to begin with.

For you, you probably know the rules. If you haven't worn something in the last year, get rid of it or pass it along. If it doesn't fit you right now, today, get rid of it. If it's ripped, stained, damaged in any way, fix it or get rid of it. Keeping my clothes under control never seems to be the problem. As I said before, I have very small closets, so I don't have much. Right now I probably have about 3 pairs of jeans, two pairs of corduroys, 1 pair of "dressy" black pants, one pair of walking/yoga/work out pants, 1 pair of motorcycle pants (reinforced for safety), 1 pair of brown suede pants and 1 pair of cranberry velvet pants. That's it. I can't wear more than one pair at a time, so why have so many. In the summer, I put all of those away except for the motorcycle pants and 1 pair of jeans. This number seems to carry me through just fine.

I have about a dozen T-shirts, (some short sleeved, some long), a few blouses, a few jackets, and a half a dozen sweaters. Rounding out my entire wardrobe are 6 or so skirts and 4 dresses. That's it. In the summer I pack away the long sleeve shirts, long pants and sweaters and bring out the short sleeve tees and light weight skirts and shorts. Now, admittedly, I don't work in an office, but see what bare essentials you can work with. Less really is more when it comes to clothes and shoes too. I have about a dozen pairs of shoes, and that seems to do it.

Day 14 – Your Families Clothing

It's the other members of the family that usually take up more space and energy. But, as with most things around the house, if you get them on a schedule, it works. Now, kids grow, so usually what fit last year won't fit this year. I have boxes of hand-me downs stored in our eves to pass down from one son to another. Since there is a five year gap in ages between my first two sons, I label the stored boxes by size (for example – size 10 -12). That way I know where everything is, and can simply pull out the next size when needed. I store the clothes in plastic bins, this way they won't rip or disintegrate like cardboard boxes would, and I can use the bins over and over.

Every spring and fall, this is what happens in my house. I take out the bin of season appropriate clothes, labeled from the previous season when I put them away (like Jeff & Adam, spring 2010, labeled in fall 2009). I go through the bin first, without anyone else around. I sort out clothes that are too small, have stains, rips or holes and in general anything I just can't stand, and get rid of it. It's important to do this while the kids aren't there, otherwise they will beg to keep the T-shirt that they outgrew over the winter. This way, nine times out of ten, they won't remember a particular article of clothing unless they see it. And they won't see it because you've removed it already. Then I take out the bin of hand me downs for whatever size the boys are now. I open it, and sort the clothes into piles for each boy, based on size. I take one boy's pile and spread it out neatly on my bed, Then, I call that boy in, and tell him to remove anything from the bed that he won't wear. Keep in mind that they have never seen these clothes before, because the last time the clothes were out of the box was 5 years ago!

I tell them to hand me anything they wouldn't wear, for whatever reason, (color, collar, pattern). When they hand me what they don't like, I put it all into a bag to donate, and then put the remainder into their closet. This way I'm not stuck with items I love but they don't. It's time to let them go to someone who actually would wear them. It also assures that everything in their closet is something they like, and have agreed to wear. Then I repeat the same process with the next son, adding in anything that his brother rejected but he would fit into. My two younger sons are completely different in what they like, so before I get rid of something, I just want to make sure neither one would wear it. If something is still in good shape, but too big, I put it into the correct stored bin for another appearance at a later date. If someone doesn't like something just because, out it goes. Why set yourself up for battles? And I admit, there were plenty of gorgeous button down shirts my first son wore that the other two rejected because they don't like anything with buttons. I simply bagged them up and donated them so they wouldn't just take up space and cause arguments in the future.

Now it's time for you to purge the excess – how many pairs of pants does a kid need anyway? What works for us is 7, one for every day of the week. If their stack is bigger then 7, I simply remove the least favorites and donate them. I do the same with shirts – 10 shirts seems to be the magic number, including long sleeve in winter, and short sleeve in summer. My boys hate sweaters, so they don't have any. They did, but I got rid of them. They take up way too much space for something they never wear. We have one or two sweatshirts, one light weight jacket, one winter jacket – that's about it. We don't have too many "dressy occasions, but I made sure they each have a collared shirt that they agreed to wear, as well as concert attire for band concerts. These are kept in a separate drawer so when concert time rolls around, they can find them. And that's about all they have – just what works for them and their needs right now.

In the warmer months, we swap out shorts for long pants, short-sleeved shirts for long sleeve, again going through the items laid out on the bed. It takes a bit longer to implement than just unpacking the clothes, but it saves time and space in the long run. And, while I am putting their clothes in their closets, I make a list of what additional items they need to bring both counts up to 7 pants and 10 shirts. That way I can make one trip to the store (or internet) and get all that's needed. At the end of the season, I also take stock for next year. For example, when packing up the winter clothes, I jot down who needs new snow pants, gloves, hats, boots, etc. Then I write that info on the monthly calendar in the September 1st space. Keep in mind it's only usually April when I am writing this (when I pack away the winter clothes), but then the info is there when I need it in September. I can get items when they are in the stores and be ready for that first snowy day. And, I can easily find it.

I do the same for summer. I write down who needs a new swim suit on the calendar for March 1st when I pack away the summer clothes in October. Granted, I don't have next year's calendar by then, but I write a note in December so I transfer it over when I get the new calendar. This works for me, and I don't have to spend any extra time thinking about it. And if I stumble upon a good sale, I know what I need. When it comes to shoes, my kids only seem to wear sneakers and snow boots, so that's all I buy. I always buy dark colors so dirt doesn't show. We also have a pair of "concert shoes". These can usually get handed down from one kid to the next since they are only worn a few times a year. That's it. Keep it simple, keep it basic, and keep only what they will wear. Your closets will thank you. (I'll talk about sports clothes and equipment later).

As for husbands, try to get them on the same page as you. Have them edit out what they don't need. Don't save anything for when they lose weight since that day may never happen, and chances are the styles will change anyway. If it's not being worn now, get rid of it. Again, your closets will thank you.

Teens? Just let them do their own thing. They will anyway, so why fight their quest for independence. Just close the door and keep out of it. It's a short period of time until they are an adult and hopefully out of your house. Let them test their wings while at home, and keep the door closed. Always closed.

4. THE ENTRYWAY

It's hard having five people all live in a small space, especially when once upon a time you used to be only responsible for yourself. Suddenly, there is stuff everywhere, and it's not your stuff! What to do, what to do? Well, you can just hope your family members will keep it neat and orderly, but honestly, you have a better chance of winning the lottery then that happening. So, you might as well set up some systems to help. Don't think of it as you taking over, but as you teaching them how to do it themselves so that they can carry on your wisdom once they leave your happy home!

So about your entryway - is it a mess? If so, how can you bear to come home each day? Doesn't it drive you crazy? What if unexpected visitors drop by? Let's tackle it. Now, it may be big, it may be small, but it needs to be orderly. Take a look at what you and your family bring in with you each day. Purse, backpacks, bags, coats, keys, mail, books, the list goes on and on. Does each of those items you bring in the door have a designated space to go? If not, there's your trouble right there. Nowhere to put things equals a big mess, day after day.

Let's take it from the top.

Day 15 – Coats

Coats, you absolutely need a place to hang your coat every day. Hooks usually work the best, but you need enough for everyone in the family. In theory, a coat closet would make sense, but usually they are so jammed packed with items that there is no way you could hang a coat in there, much less get it back out. And, after coming home from a long day, are you really going to open up a closet, pull out a hanger, hang your coat on it, replace the hanger, and then close the door? I'm betting you won't. However, if you had a row of hooks somewhere near the front door, you could just hang your coat right on a hook and be done. It's neat and orderly. It's a no brainer.

Now depending on how your front entry is laid out, you may not have room for hooks right there. I don't. Well, I do if I want to put them behind the door, but that would make for a huge clump of coats and we wouldn't be able to open the door all the way. That would be depressing, kind of like fighting your way in each day! So, instead, I have a decorative coat rack that mounts onto the wall about 6 steps away from the front door located in my den. And, I keep the access to it free and clear so that it's easier to go put the coat there instead of throwing it on the couch. It seems to work, at least for my husband and me.

For the kids I have a different system. There is another coat rack hung at their height in the kitchen. They usually seem to go into that room first anyway, so, I simply hung four different hooks on a wall with their individual photos above them to show whose hook was whose, and one extra for guests. The pictures were more important when they were young and couldn't read. Now it's just fun to see the photos there. Backpacks go on the hooks also. I don't have the space available, but if you do, you could make a whole wall with areas for each kid. In different houses we redo, I always make sure to include a mud room area or at least a wall to drop things off in. If you do have room, some cubbies for shoes are great, a bulletin board, a clock, a magnetic board , and whatever you think would work for your family and your space available. The most important thing is that you have some sort of designated space, and that it's located near where you enter your house each day. If you come in through the back door, put it there. If you come in through the garage,

74

put it there. And, a nice touch if you can swing, it is to mount the hooks/rack over a heat source, like a baseboard heater – this way coats are always warm and dry in the winter. Don't block the heat source, just mount the hooks high enough so the coats hang above the heater.

Day 16 - All the other stuff!

Okay, back to what you bring in with you; bags/purses/briefcases, etc. Again, they need a home. Ours are stored on the back of the closet door in the den. If it is something you carry every day, make a spot where only that lives. Now, I don't carry a purse, just a wallet. If I did carry a purse, I would mount a hook under the coat rack. The hook is always there and waiting for the purse, but not in the way.

How about keys? In our house, we don't have a front door key. The lock is a combination so that we never get locked out, and there are no keys to lose. I love this. The kids can always get in, even if they happen to get home before you unexpectedly. Look into this if it sounds good to you. The locks are available online. Anyway, the only keys we carry are for the car. Now, if you are the only one who uses your car, I'm guessing your keys would be in your purse. But, if you are like us and have multiple drivers using the keys, it makes sense to have them stored in a central location. We have a key cabinet mounted on the wall right next to the front door. The cabinet rests on a small wall mounted table. The table is just small enough to put something on that needs to leave the house, (library books, brownies for the bake sale), but not large enough to store anything on. In fact, the table surface is only 23" x 14", and it is a curved shape.

The key cabinet is mounted to the wall above the table, but it looks like it is sitting on the table. The cabinet is small, but has a door covering the key hooks, and a slot next to it for outgoing mail. The door holds a photo, so it is decorative as well as useful. I have our annual family photo in it. The cabinet has been there for years, and I update the photo each year. It's easy to open and hang the keys on the correct hook. If the keys are missing, you know they're in someone's pocket. (I can only set up the systems, I can't force my family to use them.) But, usually a good system works better for everyone, so they do use it. I love this combination by the front door and it makes it seems like we have a foyer, even when we don't. Like I mentioned before, we live in a Cape Cod style house – so the front door opens up directly into the living room. This table/key cabinet combo gives the feeling of another area, even when there really isn't one.

Okay, how about gloves & hats? In winter, (and early spring and fall), I rarely leave the house without a hat and gloves. I'm just always cold! So, when I come inside, I need somewhere to put them. For some people a basket works, but I always find it takes too long to locate which hats and gloves I need. So what we have, one of my favorite things, is a CD cabinet mounted directly to the wall about three steps away from the front door. The one we have was purchased at IKEA. It's made of solid wood and matches the bookcases in the den. It looks like a dresser, but it is only 7" deep. It has six "drawers" to store CD in. They're not really drawers, they are tilt out shelves, that look like drawers. Each shelf is labeled inside as to what it holds. The top shelf holds gloves, the next shelf holds hats, then kid's gloves, kids' hats and the bottom two shelves hold kid's shoes. When the kids were small, many pairs of shoes could fit inside. As they get bigger, only one pair fits per shelf. This works out fine for us, you may need a different configuration. Special cubbies are sold that mount directly to the wall and store bigger shoes. IKEA has these also.

The important thing is that there is some place to put them. Otherwise, you'll just trip over them. Anyway, the kids always take their shoes off the minute they walk into the house, and hopefully, put them in the shoe cubby. When they do, it works great since then they know where to find them the next morning. I say when they do, because nine times out of ten, I find them under the kitchen table. (The shoes, not the kids). At least when I tell them to put their shoes away, there is a place for them. It's usually a lonely, empty place, but hey, at least it's a place. Not all systems can work perfectly! My husband and I usually keep our shoes on in the house. It doesn't matter what your family does, just create a system and a place for whatever works for you and your family.

What else do we carry in to the house? Bags – filled with purchases. I try to only use reusable bags. When they are unpacked, they are folded up and put on the small table by the front door. The next person out to the car puts them back into the car trunk, ready for next time. Since the table is right next to the front door, and there is nothing else on it except the bags, it's hard to ignore them when you walk out the door. So, they usually get put back into car, waiting for the next shopping trip. Any plastic bags brought inside get stored in a fabric chicken hanging from the ceiling in the kitchen above the sink. Yes, I said in the "chicken". Really, it's just one of those fabric tubes sold in catalogs used especially for the purpose of storing plastic bags. It's easy to put the bag in, and easy to get one out when needed. For some strange reason, my cats like to chew on the plastic bags, so it's better for all if they are stored out of the cat's reach.

Now for something that quickly takes over your home.

Day 17 – Sports Equipment

How about sports equipment? Now, depending on your family, you may need an entire room for this! You need to take stock of what always seems to be lying around and figure out how to store it. For us, we're a baseball family. That's our only "organized" sport. So, we have bats, ball, gloves, catcher's equipment and such to store. For the big stuff, I have a large plastic chest in the back yard. It's one of those Rubbermaid outdoor containers. It's not the prettiest thing to look at, but it does store a lot of stuff. When we come home from baseball, I send the boys right to the back yard to drop off the bats and catcher's equipment into the chest. Balls and gloves get stored inside for easy access.

We have a square footstool that also has storage in it. I keep it in the den and it's just the right size for baseball gloves and a few balls. Easy to put them in, and easy to take them out. The boys' baseball pants and such are usually stored here also. It works for us. All you really have to do is see what you have, where it gets used, and create some storage for it. And, remember to get rid of old equipment when it is no longer needed. For example, we only keep the current season's baseball cap, the others get given away. Don't keep it if you don't use it!

And while we are on the topic of sports equipment, don't store out of season equipment anywhere you will see it when that sport is not being played. Put it somewhere out of sight. We store ice skates, swimming goggles and such under the steps in the basement. Each sport has its own cubby so we can find them when needed, but they aren't in the way. If you have space in your garage, getting a system specially designed to hold sports equipment is the way to go. "A place for everything, and everything in its place". They have these systems everywhere now. Just break down and install one. You will be thanking yourself over and over again when baseball bats are not propped up by the kitchen door, waiting to trip you up when you come home.

That's it for the entryway. On to the next area......

5. THE LIVING ROOM / FAMILY ROOM

Our living room is the heart of our home. We don't have a family room as such, so the living room is where all of our living takes place. This means TV viewing, homework, guests visiting, playing board games, playing TV games, reading, napping, playing with toys and passing through to the kitchen. It all happens here. And this room is small, maybe 13' x 15'. It's the main entryway into the house. It's the first area people see. And in my house, it's always neat and orderly. How can this be you may ask? Because everything has its place.

Okay, let's see what I have in the living room. We already talked about the small wall mounted table by the front door. It's worth its weight in gold. There is also a leather sofa. Leather because it's easy to keep clean and almost indestructible. I don't want to spend my time telling the kids to be careful all day, so everything we own has to be durable and useable. This leather couch is both. I strongly recommend dark colored leather furniture if you have kids. Spills don't soak in, pet hair doesn't get stuck, but toys do still show up on it, so......

Day 18 – Toy Storage

Where there are kids, there are toys. And they seem to be taking over the house! And the amount keeps growing whenever you turn your back! Now, I have to admit as the kids get bigger, the toys do get smaller. But I've dealt with my fair share of kids' storage. Did I mention I used to do family day care out of my home? For five years, my house looked like a day care center, but it also was neat and orderly. Here are some of my ideas.

Toys come in all shapes and sizes, that's what makes them so difficult to store. We keep a lot of toys in the living room, but they are not easily seen. How you may ask? Well, I have built in bookshelves next to my fireplace. When we bought the house, the previous owners displayed a few knick-knacks there. We use the space for storage. I bought wicker baskets from IKEA that fit perfectly on the shelf, and each basket holds one type of toy, (blocks in one, tinker toys in another). I never keep the original boxes the toys came in. They don't stand up to normal wear and tear. Instead, the baskets work wonderfully. Some baskets are tall, some are short, but they all have the same front to them. This way when they are stored on the shelf they all look the same. Your eye just glides over them. You see them as a solid, not a bunch of different colors and shapes, so it looks calm and orderly. When the kids were younger and didn't like to put things away, I had each spot on the shelf labeled with which basket goes where. And, there was a photo of the toy also. I just took a picture of the actual toy with my camera, printed it out, mounted it to a piece of paper, and then wrote the name of the toy underneath the photo. This also helps with reading skills). Then I would cover the whole thing in clear contact paper, leaving a half-inch border all around. I would peel off the paper and stick the photo/name tag right on the shelf, and then put the basket on top of it.

This way, the nametags are hidden when the basket is on top, but are easy to see when the basket is not on the shelf. Hiding the label under the basket makes the living room look neat when guests come over. No need to see the tricks! Doing it this way, it was like a game for the kids to put the baskets back on the correct shelf, Any kid visitors could easily help clean up when playtime was over. Again, the key is to have a place for everything. Down in the basement we have a version of the same system. We just have bigger cubbies (they didn't all have to match). We bought some inexpensive wire shelving, the type you put together to make cubes. One cubby or one toy fit into each cube, that way it was easy to clean up. The nametag was hung from the top of the cube with paperclips. And, if there were too many toys for the cubes, it was time to either get rid of some of them, or start doing toy rotation.

Toy rotation, what's that you may ask? Well, this was a great idea when the kids were small. Basically, I would pack away a good portion of the toys in boxes and put them into deep storage somewhere. Then, about six months later, I would bring them out, let the kids unpack the boxes, and it was like Christmas all over again. The original toys would go into storage, only to reappear six months later. And if you still have too many toys around, you could store more and bring them out quarterly or so, whatever works for you. This makes everyone happy. You'll have fewer toys to trip over on a daily basis, and the kids get "new" toys every few months. The unpacking and repacking of the toys can fill up an entire morning, and the kids love it! I would mark the date on the calendar so they could look forward to it.

Since my youngest boys are now 10 and 12, we don't rotate toys anymore, but the more I think about it, maybe we should start again because the toys are taking over again!

Day 19 – Electronic Toys

What about electronic toys? These take over the house quicker than anything else does. CD's, DVD's, video's, game cartridges......where to put them, how to store them? If you are like me you hate to see them just lying around. I can't tell you how much money was wasted due to scratched discs. Whenever I saw them just lying on the floor I would go crazy! So, something had to be done. I was threatening to get rid of all of it, but I was out voted on that score. So, a system needed to be introduced. Now, I'm happy to say, we actually seem to have one that works, and I rarely find any lying around. Here's the system:

CD's – we purchased a CD player that you can download the CD directly into. I have absolutely no idea how it works, but it does. Basically, any CD we have gets fed into this machine, I press the button that says STORE, and the machine stores all of the music. I remove the CD, and put it into a notebook with CD inserts. The CD inserts are those pages that fit into a loose-leaf notebook, and hold CD's and DVD's. You can find them at any office supply store. Then the notebook gets stored in some out of the way place, since you no longer need the actual CD to listen to music.

Now, whenever I want to hear a specific CD, I use the remote to look through the machine's menu, and then just press a button. This works great because I can browse by artist, CD title, or specific song. Whoever invented this machine was brilliant! However, if you want to stick with the CD player you have, just use the notebook system. Both systems require you to take a leap of faith and GET RID OF THE JEWEL BOXES! (Those are the plastic boxes the CD's came in.) Now, for some people, they feel this is wrong, wrong, wrong. These are also the same people that save everything. Think about it, it's just a plastic box. Yes, the liner notes may be important to some people, but you can always store these in the notebook along with the CD's. But, if this seems crazy to you, you can pack the empty jewel boxes up and put them into deep storage until a later date when you see they are useless and are ready to toss them.

Now, though I was ready to dump the jewel boxes the first time one came into my house, my husband was not.

So, gradually we worked towards storing just the CD's. The boxes we kept in deep storage for a while, until one day I was on line at IKEA waiting to pay, and in front of me was a man trying to buy some empty jewel cases. Unfortunately, for him, the boxes were just for display. The cashier said everyone tries to buy them. I realized a win/win situation was presenting itself. I offered him all of my stored jewel boxes! I got his name and address, and sent them all to him. He was happy, I was happy, and my husband, after a bit of convincing, realized that the boxes were better off being used somewhere than sitting in our eave taking up space. He hasn't missed them since!

Now, we do have a few lightweight CD holders that we use to transport CD's to the car, but no more sliding, easily broken jewel boxes. And all of our CD's fit into a much, much, much smaller space than before, even if you count storing the loose-leaf notebook. And, a great benefit is that I can rent CD's from the library, download them to store them, and return the original CD. Then there is nothing to store and it costs nothing!

DVD's. Now, sadly to say, such a machine doesn't exist yet for DVD's. There seem to be some sort of copyright laws according to my husband. Anyway, we've come up with a system that works. It's a bit of a long explanation, so bear with me here. Now, in front of our couch in the living room we have an ottoman that doubles as a coffee table. It measures 25" x 20", and it opens for storage. (Rule of life here is to never, ever, ever buy an ottoman or footstool that doesn't open for storage. It's a complete waste of space otherwise!) So, the ottoman opens for storage. This is where all of our DVD's are kept neatly, not just tossed in. I purchased some DVD holders from Staples that are kind of like small zip closed leather cases. I'm sure they have a name, but I just call them DVD holders. They unzip, open flat and four DVD's just slip right in per page. You do have to get rid of the jewel boxes again. (Maybe you can find someone like my guy from IKEA, or list them on Craig's List for free. There are plenty of people in the world who haven't figured out yet that they are just a big waste of space.)

Anyway, back to the holders. They have a handle on the back for easy transport. They are all exactly the same size, all fit exactly into the footstool, nestled up against each other, with their spines facing up with the handles easily accessible. Each DVD holder stores 100 DVD's and five holders fit nicely into the space in the footstool, with room left over. Each holder is labeled. There is a space for a label on the handle. We have categories such as kids, dramas, comedies, musicals, etc. Chose whatever categories work for you. Inside each holder is that type of genre, in alphabetical order. It takes a bit of time to set it up, but then it works great.

Let's say you want to watch Ocean's Eleven. You would open up the footstool, take out the case labeled comedies, flip to the O section, and there it would be. And when you are done, it's easy to put it back since there is an open space for it in the holder. Teenagers seem to like to sort the DVD's out, so this is a perfect job for them! And speaking of teens, my older son has his own much bigger case that he stores in his room. When we want to borrow a DVD, it's pretty easy to find it, and that's saying something in a teen's room! The cases also make it easy to travel with DVD's. For a while, we had a car with a DVD player in it, so on long trips the boys could just grab their holder of DVD's and be ready to go. We are experiencing a bit of disparity now with the advent of Blue Ray discs that come with three discs a piece, but so far, the system is still working. And we can store 500 DVD's in a very small space, and rest our feet on it also. Perfect multitasking.

Videos. Luckily, these are going the way of the dinosaurs, but we still have some floating around. I simply have them lined up on a low bookshelf, but I'm always trying to pare them down. Eventually they will disappear. Until then I just live with it.

Game cartridges & discs. These are small. And so expensive that you can't really own a lot. Anyway, we keep them in their original boxes, lined up on a bookshelf.

They don't seem to be taking over, and the kids seem to keep track of them. Computer games and WII games are also kept in their original boxes, but they could just as easily be kept in a loose-leaf notebook or DVD holder. We keep them in the boxes because my teen usually trades them on line for new games, so the original boxes are needed. All of the equipment that goes with these games is kept in the same footstool in front of the couch. Remember when I said there was room left over? This is what fits in there, assorted wires, add-ons, etc. The actual WII remotes get stored in their chargers near an outlet. At least they look neat, though they wouldn't be my first choice in tabletop accessories. And one of the wicker baskets on the living room shelves stores the small hand held games like Game Boys and such. They are easy to find, and I don't have to look at them all the time.

Day 20 – Books

Books. It seems that people either haves lots and lots of them, or hardly any at all. I love books. I read all of the time. I go through at least a novel a week. Not to mention self-help books, business books, cook books. We seem to have a lot of books. The kids have books, my husband has books. We have ended up with our own mini library. So, here's how to keep them organized. Obviously, you need bookshelves. Good, solid wood bookshelves. No particle board shelves or MDF (medium density fiberboard). After all, books weigh a lot, and you don't want sagging shelves. A bit more invested now will pay off in the long run. We have two bookcases in the den with five shelves each. The boys have one in their room, and my teen has one in his room. Some of my cookbooks get stored in the kitchen in an old desk with glass doors. The rest are on the shelves in the den. Periodically, I go through all the books and get rid of ones that no longer interest me.

Titles like healthy microwave cooking, is there really such a thing?

I attempt to have my husband get rid of reference books from 1965 and such. It doesn't always work. Now, it's very important to let family members decide what books they want to get rid of. Never, ever pare down someone's book collection for them. That's just asking for trouble. At least once a year I send the boys to their rooms to go through their books and make a pile to donate. (More about this later.) As long as you keep on top of it, and give the books a place to live, it seems to work.

However, you do need to utilize the new one in, old one out principle. Otherwise, you will be drowning. A brilliant way to avoid this is to simply not buy any more books. Instead, I borrow the books from the library. Our library system is all computerized, so when I find out about a book I'm interested in reading, either from a friend, a magazine or the newspaper, I go on line and check if our library system has it. Nine times out of ten they do. Then I place a hold order via the computer, and within a week, the book is waiting for me at the library. I do this with all the fiction books I read. I also do it with how to and nonfiction books. Then only if the book has vital info I need, do I purchase the book. And nine times out of ten, I can get what I need from the book without purchasing it. There are less things to store at my house, and a wide world of books open to me at no charge. It can't get better then that! If you don't frequent your library at least once a week, start doing so! The amount of materials available, whether books, CD's, DVD's, lectures or classes available at no cost is amazing.

We're almost there!

Day 21 – Components

Yes, I'm talking about all those machines needed to run the DVD's, CD's, games, etc. This has got to be the bane of my existence, and the place where my husband and I disagree the most. I feel that we could get along with only the bare minimum needed in the way of equipment. He feels just the opposite. And he's a techno geek, always keeping up with what's current and best. So, as a result, we have many components. I have no idea what most of them do. And, I admit it, I don't even want to know what they do. I just want them to work. Why can't you just plug something in and it works? It seems that most equipment doesn't even come with cables to plug it in. I swear, sometimes I think it's done on purpose just to drive me crazy!

Anyway, the biggest "problem" we had in our living room was the giant flat screen TV. I bet I'm not alone in this. I can't stand it being the focal point of the (very small) room. My husband is fine with it being the first thing you see when you walk in the front door. Yikes, what to do? We came to an agreement. The TV needed to be easily accessible for him (and my boys, like father, like son), but easily hidden for me. Years ago, before flat screens, the TV armoire solved this problem. No more. Now with flat screen TV's, the TV is front and center again. So here's what we did. Before installing the set, we researched different ways of making it less obtrusive. And there are ways out there, from rolling screens to fully automated systems whose sole purpose is to hide the screen. And they all cost a fortune, some more than the cost of the set! This was obviously out of the question.

So, I thought about it for a bit, and came up with the perfect answer. It's cheap, easy to use, and low tech. Our TV is mounted on the wall over the fireplace. It's great that it takes up no floor space, but not so great in that it is the width of the fireplace. Now remember, my living room is only about 12' x 14, and this is the main focal wall. I absolutely hated the big black screen calling "turn me on, turn me on" whenever it wasn't turned on. We needed to conceal it, and fast. So, I measured the size of the actual screen, and then ordered a blank art canvas in that size. I actually ordered the stretcher strips and stretched my own canvas, but you can order a stretched canvas either online or at an art supply store. Then, I painted a picture right on the canvas. You don't have to be an artist to do this. You could simply paint an abstract with colors you like. Anything will work. You could even just stretch a piece of decorative fabric on the stretcher strips. I actually divided the canvas into six smaller squares so that it wouldn't overpower the room, and then painted a different flower scene on each one. Once this was all dry, my husband made some metal hooks the depth of the TV exactly, and we attached the hooks onto the back of the canvas. You could also buy over the door closet hooks that would work, even a pair of wreath hangers with the bottoms cut off would solve the problem. When the TV is not on, the canvas hangs right over the screen, and when the TV is on, you simply lift the canvas down and hang it on the molding on the front of the fireplace. It's not heavy at all, and it doesn't hurt the TV at all. The kids can even do it by themselves. And the best part is, no one who walks into our house even realizes there is a TV there. It simply looks like a painting hanging on the wall.

I'm happy, he's happy, and all parts of the problem were solved. If your TV isn't on the wall, you could easily do the same concept. Just make the canvas into smaller panels and it could act like a folding screen sitting on a tabletop. It would look decorative when you want, and would be easy to remove when you wanted to use the TV.

All of our other equipment is contained in a large cabinet bought especially for this purpose. It has doors on the front, so it can be closed up when not in use. Our cabinet had clear glass doors when we bought it, but that did nothing to hide the clutter inside, so I simply covered the inside of the doors with some frosted contact paper. Again, it's easy to get to everything, but isn't sitting out to contribute to the clutter. My husband actually mounted the entire cabinet on wheels so that when he needs to rewire something, the whole cabinet wheels out easily.

And, if you still have old, obsolete equipment sitting in your house, it's time to get rid of it. Trust me, 8 tracks are never coming back. If you don't use it, get rid of it. Sell it if you want and use the money to buy more storage cubbies. Or go out to dinner, your choice!

Day 22 – Mail & Paperwork

Mail. It is hard to believe the amount of mail we get each day in our house. Bills, catalogs, ads, but hardly ever any real letters! How do you tame this mess? First of all, remove your name from junk mail lists. The Direct Marketing Association is the group that gives your name and address to companies. Just let them know you don't want your name given out. Write to them at: Mail Preference Service, Attn: Dept. 6150403, Direct Marketing Association, P.O. Box 282 Carmel, NY 10512. Once removed, your name will stay off their list for five years. You can also do it online, but it will cost you. Writing is free, except for the cost of the stamp.

Keep in mind that if you order online or through the mail, you will probably receive that company's catalog in the mail. So if you don't want to receive the catalog, call the company and ask them to remove you from their mailing list. It takes about three months, but eventually your amount of junk mail will lessen.

This should cut down on your junk mail. But what about all that important stuff you get in the mail, like bills? How can you keep track of them without losing them under piles? First off, recycle anything you don't need. Set up a very large bag to put recycling into, and then sort your mail directly over or next to this place. Anything you don't need goes right into the recycling. This includes envelopes after you've opened up the important mail, as well as things you don't ever need to look at. Just get rid of it. If you glance at it, then put it aside for later to decide if you really need it. It will be in your house for a very long time. Decide as soon as you see it! Now you should have a manageable pile left. Boring things like bills or anything you need to take care of should go into something you go through each week. I use the treasure chest on my kitchen counter. This way nothing gets lost. Fun things, like magazines and such that I want to read later, go into a decorative bin that sits on top of a low bookcase in the living room. This way I can locate any magazine quickly since I can see them.

When reading a magazine, I sit down with a red pen and circle anything I'm interested in. I circle names of books I want to request from the library, internet sites I want to check out, ideas I want to try, recipes etc. Then I rip the page out and put in into the treasure chest on my kitchen counter. Once a week when I sort the papers in the chest, these pages are put into a "check on computer" pile. Then I go to the computer and research the websites, order books from the library, etc. Once I'm done with the magazine, I either recycle it or pass it on to a friend. If I'm passing it on, I don't rip out pages, I just make note of websites, etc. Usually a magazine lasts in my house only a few days before it is recycled or passed along. Again, it cuts down on the clutter.

Recipes, once they are family taste tested and approved they are filed in an ordinary photo book. You know those small ones that hold one photo per page. I took one with a kitchen theme, and divided it into sections using some of those small sticky note reminder flags. They act like dividers for the sections. Then I labeled the sections, beef, chicken, pork, etc. This way it is easy to slip a new recipe into the book, and I can find it when I need it. It also helps when planning menus for the week. If I need a chicken dish, all my chicken recipes are in one place. And if I run out of room in the book, I do not get another book. I simply go through my current one, and discard recipes we no longer use. Remember, if it's not being used, it doesn't belong in your house. It doesn't matter how small or large the item is. If it's not needed, out it goes!

Day 23 – Storage

I don't think I can ever have enough storage. There are so many cute things in the world, and you just want to own all of them. But ask yourself this important question before you buy anything, where am I going to put it? If you don't know, don't buy it.

Now, certain things just happen, like holiday decorations. Christmas decorations obviously need some bins of their own that get stored in deep storage. But what about Halloween, Valentine's Day, 4th of July? All those decorations don't take up much space by themselves, but when added all together, space becomes precious. Here's what works for me. I recycled some large diaper boxes by covering them with contact paper, and put labels on the outside. It looks decorative, but stays neat, and family members can find things. Then I outfitted my one coat closet with shelves. These boxes fit perfectly on the shelves. And if the closet is accidently left open, they look fine. I have boxes for holiday decorations, donations, and candles. I used to have one for gift-wrap, but recently I moved that, (more about that later). In the holiday decoration box are individual large zip locks with all the decorations for specific holidays. This way, when it's time to decorate, I can easily pull out what we need and be sure I have all of it.

In the donation box, I put all the items we no longer need. When the box is full, I bag it up and take it to my local thrift shop. Again, it keeps things orderly, accessible, and it's easy to slip things into the box. If I had to walk around trying to figure out where to put things I wanted to donate, I would never do it! Making it easy works for me. And speaking of donations, if you happen to be someone who loves to hold onto items, ask yourself a few questions when deciding if you should get rid of something. Wouldn't it be better if the item was with someone who would actually use it? What's the worst that could happen if you got rid of it? I donate items all of the time, and I can honestly say I've never regretted getting rid of anything. Once it's gone, you will never think about it or trip over it again.

In the candle box I keep candles and all the accessories that go with them. I tend to swap out different candles depending on the season, so the box gives me a place to store them. And, I burn them too!

I use to have a box with gift wrap supplies in it, but I recently realized that it was no longer functioning for me. Originally, when I set up the system I had a large empty counter top next to the closet. (Actually, I used a counter top for changing diapers. After cleaning it a zillion times a day with anti-bacterial wipes and bleach, I figured it would work for gift-wrapping also.) And this worked great, for a while. Now to show you how even an organized person can still be doing unorganized things, I recently realized that the system no longer works because there is no longer a counter next to the closet. When I needed to wrap a gift, I would take down the box, walk it through three rooms to get to a table I could wrap on, and then walk it back. And I had ribbon hanging on the inside of the closet door, so that would mean another trip back for ribbon. All this walking was silly, especially when I realized that I had been doing this for years! My youngest is ten years old. It's been quite a while since he was in diapers, so quite a while since there was a counter there! And yet, I kept walking across three rooms. ...

Anyway, just a few weeks ago I moved my gift-wrapping supplies down to the basement. I have a small counter there that I use to fold laundry on. This space has shelves that weren't being used too wisely, and a bulletin board left from my sewing days. So, what I did was turn this space into a gift wrapping area. Rolls of gift-wrap are stored on shelf supports, gift bags are hung on cup hooks in the wall, and spools of ribbon are on a dowel hung up so the ribbon can spool off of it. On the shelves, I filled some decorative boxes with gift tags, bows, etc. I hung a few family photos on the bulletin board, along with nails to hold scissors and tape. All in all, the area looks great now, functions beautifully. I only fold laundry once a day, so the counter is empty the rest of the time. I certainly don't wrap gifts and fold laundry at the same time, so it multitasks for both wonderfully. An extra-added benefit is the rest of the family can now wrap gifts as needed without any help from me! A win – win situation for all!

How about board games? Where do you put all of those boxes? The answer is - you don't keep the boxes! This one tip really gives you lots of extra space. This is what you do. Go to where you now keep your games, armed with a box of heavy-duty zip lock bags, a permanent marker, and a big basket of some sort. Grab a game, sit down, open the box, and take out the pieces. On the back of the game board, use the permanent marker to write the name of the game. Write the name of the game on a zip lock bag. Put all of the game pieces into the bag. Seal the bag; put the bag into the big basket, and put the board aside. Throw out the box. Now, this might sound a bit drastic to you, but trust me on this. After going through all of your games, you will be able to store them in a fraction of the space it used to take up. When you are all done, put the basket back on the shelves where you used to store the games, and stack the game boards on another shelf. Look at all the room you have left over!

An added bonus to this method is that if you are missing a piece to one game, the bags are right there and easy to browse through to find something you can use as a replacement piece. We keep some games in the living room and some in the basement. They're easy to access, and easy to use. This works with puzzles also. Just cut off the front of the puzzle box so you know what it looks like, and then put all the puzzle pieces into the bag, along with the front piece you cut off. Voila! All the puzzles will fit into a basket easily, yet the kids can locate what they want quickly. Easy, easy, easy!

6. THE GREAT OUTDOORS

I'm always amazed at how quickly the back yard gets cluttered with stuff. How can that be? Where does it come from? And where am I going to put it? And, how can my yard work with me and not against me?

Day 24 – Grass

This might be a bit radical for some of you – time to rethink your yard!

Make your life simpler by eliminating any extra grass you may have. We have no grass at all. Yep, I mean it, not a blade. And I live in the suburbs where grass is king! Having no grass saves me work, and it's better for the environment because I don't have to fertilize it, water it, or pollute the air by cutting it. How is this possible? Well, at my house we did it bit by bit. First, we built a deck in our backyard. This removed a chunk of grass. Then we sectioned off a part to be a play yard for the kids. This area was covered in 6" deep of wood chips, which removed another section of grass. Then we made a built in sandbox and covered the grass between it and the deck with more decking. This left only a small bit of grass that eventually wouldn't grow anyway. So, we removed the divider between the play yard and the remaining grass, covered it all with landscape fabric, and wood chipped the entire yard. There is still plenty of green surrounding the area, bushes, perennials, and trees. No grass and no mowing for us.

In the front yard, we covered all the grass with pea gravel. This made more parking for visitors, and a place to turn around so we don't need to back out into the street. It actually lightens up the whole front of the house. We have huge trees, so with the grass that used to be there, the entire front was very dark. The pea gravel lightened it all up, made the front area much more useful, and made it function better for us. I can't tell you how much time we save every spring and summer by not mowing. Every few years we need to top off the wood chips and pea gravel, but we still come out ahead in the cost and time factor.

Day 25 – Deck Area

As I said before, we entertain quite a bit. So, one of the first things we did when we moved in was to build a deck. We put in some built in planters and built in benches to make things easier. Across one of the benches, I laid a large plank of wood, actually a plank from scaffolding. I painted it with a checkerboard pattern, and this is what we use for a sideboard to put food on during parties. The bench below gives lots of room to put bottles of soda and such. You could also put a cooler here, but a few years ago, we simply built a cooler into the bench itself. Our benches had storage beneath them, so my husband cut a lid out of the top of the bench, and then we installed a large tub flush with the opening. We insulated it by putting foam tubes around it, and then cut a small drainage hole in the bottom of the tub. We plugged up the hole with an old-fashioned bathtub drain stopper. My husband screwed down a decorative dog statue as a handle to the lid. Now we have a built in cooler! For parties we simply fill it up with ice, and drinks, and put the lid on. If you didn't know it was a cooler, you would never know. It takes up no room at all, and is ready to go whenever we need it. It really keeps things cool also, I've checked the day after a party and things are still cold. When it comes time to drain it, we just pull out the plug. The water drains away under the deck. No muss, no fuss!

On our deck, we also keep a small plastic box filled with placemats, candles, salt and pepper, and things that we need on the picnic table when we eat outside, but don't need to be washed. I got tired of ferrying everything out from the kitchen every time we wanted to eat, so instead I now simply store the necessary items outside. A few years ago, we switched from paper plates and throwaway cups and utensils to plastic reusable ones. These get stored in a decorative black metal rack with a handle on a table right near the door to the outside. This way when they come out of the dishwasher it's easy to put them back into the rack for the next trip outside. The handle makes it easy to carry.

Day 26 – Kids Area

This has changed over the years as the kids have gotten bigger. Our yard is tiny, but we use every inch of it. We built a sandbox into the end of the deck, which makes it easy for the kids to get to. Someday it will become a fountain. We have a small swing set/play fort, a secret passage next to the deck, a few sitting areas, and a table and chairs for eating. This year I hope to put in an area with two large relaxing type chairs. Since we live next to a university, we could set them up to look over the large empty field and watch the deer at sunset. Last year this area held a swing, but the since kids are bigger now they don't need it anymore. It was time to rethink the area. Since our yard is kind of an "L" shape, I put a hammock at the corner of the L. This way I could sit in the hammock and keep an eye on kids on both ends of the yard.

And, when the kids were still in diapers, I would keep a supply of diapers and wipes in an old mailbox mounted in the yard. It was weatherproof, handy, and I wouldn't have to go inside to change one of them. Now the box is still there, but it holds garden tools. Again, it's easy to get to, it's weatherproof, and decorative. We also have a large plastic bin that the kids keep their baseball bats and such in. It's not the nicest on the eyes, but it functions well. Since there is a place for everything outside, when it's time to clean up the yard, it's pretty easy. (Just like inside.) See, it doesn't matter how small your yard is, you can make it a haven for kids and adults alike with just a little planning. Think about what you need and create it!

7 THE THINGS THAT DON'T FIT INTO ANY OTHER CATEGORY

All of those things that don't seem to fit anywhere else. We all have them - now we just need to organize them!

Day 27 – Entertaining

Well, since you now have a place for everything and everything is in its place at your house, entertaining becomes easy. No longer do you have to race around putting things away. Last minute guests mean you may have to ask your child to move their Lego bins out of the living room, but that's about it. There are no more stacks of paper and piles of stuff. Entertaining becomes easy. And to make it even easier, I suggest you purchase supplies to streamline your preparation. No more paper and plastic, instead buy some sets of all-purpose wine glasses, glass plates, dessert plates, and whatever you may need.

Set aside a storage area for these items, and whenever you entertain all you will have to think about is what to serve. We currently have 24 glass dinner plates, 36 wine glasses, 24 all-purpose glasses, silverware for 24, 36 small dessert plates, 24 glass mugs, 24 champagne glasses, and 12 martini glasses. You get the idea. These are not our everyday items, they are used only for parties. This assortment seems to cover most any type of gathering. And, any party you have will be much nicer for your guests and the environment if you don't use disposable items. And it saves you time and money by not having to purchase these items over and over again. For backyard parties, I have plastic glasses and plastic plates. These are the same ones we use for everyday dinners outside. Reusable items don't take up much storage space, just a few shelves. Entertaining becomes much easier. The landfills will thank you.

We also designed a removable coat rack for indoors. My husband installs a long pole from the top of one bookcase to another across the room in our den. A leg supports it in the middle. It only takes a few minutes to screw it to the top of the bookcases, and it can easily hold dozens of coats. I purchased plastic hangers that are only used for this coat rack They get stored hanging on a rod in the basement when not in use. Some years the rack goes up around Halloween, and doesn't come down again until after The Super Bowl! It definitely makes life easier......

8. KEEPING THINGS THIS WAY

How can you keep things this way? How can you keep things neat? Even if you are on board with your new systems and procedures, how can you get your family to cooperate?

Day 28 – Family Help

This is one of my favorite tips! It always seemed like I was the one doing all of the straightening up around my house. The kids would take something out, I would put it away. My husband would take something out, and I would put it away.

Or worse, I would be vacuuming while they were lying around watching television. This drove me crazy! I finally realized that I was doing them no favors by teaching them to expect others to clean up after them. I needed to teach them how to do it, without me nagging them about it. Assigning chores didn't seem to work. I was just always reminding them about what needed to be done. And, it was still never done. Finally, I'd had it. I realized that I resented them not helping, and more importantly, not helping willingly. Something had to change! So, I came up with "The Family Clean Up" system. Three nights a week at 7:30 pm, we all participate in a family clean up.

Everyone picks a job they want to do, and they do it. Currently our job roster consists of one person dusting, one person doing a quick vacuuming, one person cleaning the bathrooms, and two people de-cluttering. I ring the dinner bell, and first responders get the first choice of chores. The last one present gets whatever chore is left. This helps make sure everyone reports quickly. After picking their chore, each family member goes off to complete it. (First I had to teach them how to do the different jobs, but the few minutes it took really saves time in the long run.) Surprisingly enough, one of my sons always picks cleaning the bathrooms! This way we are all working together, the kids don't think the house magically stays clean, they learn how to do the jobs, and I don't resent all of them for not helping. The whole process takes about 15 minutes. Now, this does just a surface cleaning, but it seems to be enough to carry us through until I can get to the full house vacuuming and the cleaning of the bathrooms. Day 30 is approaching!

Day 29 – You

If you are like me, it helps to schedule "cleaning the bathrooms" and "vacuuming the whole house" into your weekly schedule. Otherwise, they never seem to get done, and then I feel guilty about it. If I know I will get to the bathrooms on Friday morning, I can easily sit and read a bit on a Thursday afternoon. The same goes for full house vacuuming. As long as it's on the schedule, it seems to get done. And if I miss it occasionally, it doesn't really matter. The family clean up takes care of it well enough until I can get to it the next week. Now, everyone has their own cleaning standards, so don't worry about how your friends do it, just do what works for you. I myself have no problem mopping the kitchen floor once a week, but I've heard of people who mop it once a day. Whatever levels of cleanliness work for you and your family are the correct ones. After all, no matter how clean or neat you get something, it will just get dirty again, so don't stress too much about it.

Day 30 – TAA DAA!

Look around you! Do you see a difference? Does your whole outlook seem rosier? I know that when my house is neat, my thoughts are calmer and more focused. The little things don't bother me as much. So, take a few really deep breaths and congratulate yourself. You did it! And even if you only made one change, it is a victory. Because one change will lead to another and another. Remember, it's not how much you get done that really counts, it's the fact that you started making changes. After all, tomorrow, next week, next month, and next year will all come about whether you do any organizing or not, so you might as well do a bit to help yourself in the long run. You deserve it, and you can do it, one step at a time, one day at a time.

Now, you are armed with 30 Days To An Organized Home. Go get started and organize something! Good luck and enjoy your newly discovered free time!

8. SOME USEFUL WEBSITES

In no particular order-

www.lillianvernon.com- Lillian Vernon - decorative boxes, wire dish racks

www.CuisinartWebstore.com- pots & pans

www.Brother-USA.com- label makers

www.crockpot365.blogspot.com- crock pot recipes, including the macaroni & cheese from dry pasta

www.Vitamix.com- Vita-Mix high speed blender

www.kitchensource.com/trash- pull out trash cans – all shapes and sizes *www.amazon.com*– wall mount hair dryer

www.keylessentrylocks.com– combination door locks

www.CoatRacks.com– coat racks

www.target.com– wall mounted wooden key cabinets

www.Ikea.com– wall mounted shoe cabinets or cd cabinets to use as shoe cubbies, wicker storage baskets, toy cubbies

www.rubbermaid.com– outdoor storage cubbies, toy cubbies

www.wholesaleArtsFrames.com– pre-stretched canvas

www.greaterlivingfoods.com– organic meats

And last but not least. . .

www.ebay.com– if you search in EBay under "chicken plastic bag holder" you will find a variety of them – while this isn't exactly the one I have, it will definitely work. You can get a pig one also!

From Evelyn......

Congratulations!

You've taken major steps towards getting your home to work for you, instead of you working for your home. By now you've hopefully de-cluttered some major messes and have created more free time to do the things you really want to do. And hopefully my instructions were clear.

Want more?

Just go to

http://www.TheHopefulLife.com

and join my world. There you'll find my blog, and all sorts of ways to make your life easier.

be efficient & organized......

Evelyn

ABOUT THE AUTHOR

Evelyn Cucchiara used to think she was an organizer.

But she's not. She's much more than that.

She's an efficiency expert. She can look at a problem area in any home and design a system to correct it. Permanently. And usually with less effort then it took to keep it messy.

She believes that uncluttered homes lead to uncluttered lives. And she's on a mission to bring back the calm, peaceful family life of yesteryear.

She is a sought after public speaker, teleseminar presenter and webinar creator. Find out more about the products, workshops, books, her blog and services she offers at http://www.TheHopefulLife.com and find out how to make your life happy, organized, profitable, efficient & full. The Hopeful Life.

Evelyn is a lifelong resident of New Jersey, where she lives with her boys, her husband of 3 decades and two cats. She is the creator and founder of Art Adventures, http://www.artadventuresartstudio.com, a children's art studio that she has run out of her home for over a dozen years.

Notes

Notes

Notes

Notes

Notes

Notes

Notes